rockschool®

I0811159

Piano

US Level 5 (UK Grade 5)

Performance pieces, technical exercises, supporting tests and in-depth guidance for Rockschool assessments

All accompanying and supporting audio can be downloaded from: *www.rslawards.com/downloads*

Input the following code when prompted: **3HFXB248RZ**

For more information, turn to page 5

www.rslawards.com

Acknowledgements

Published by Rockschool Ltd. © 2019 & 2020
Catalogue Number: RSK200094US
ISBN: 978-1-78936-170-4
Initial US Release | Errata details can be found at *www.rslawards.com/errata*

SYLLABUS
Syllabus designed and written by Jono Harrison
Syllabus Director: Tim Bennett-Hart
Syllabus consultants: Gary Sanctuary, Chris Stanbury, Simon Troup and Jennie Troup
Hit Tune arrangements by Jono Harrison and Gary Sanctuary
Supporting Tests written by Jono Harrison, Chris Stanbury, Nik Preston and Ash Preston
Syllabus advisors: Tim Bennett-Hart, Brian Ashworth, Stuart Slater, Peter Huntington, Bruce Darlington, Simon Troup and Jennie Troup

PUBLISHING
Proof reading of arrangements by Sharon Kelly, Simon Troup, Jennie Troup and Jono Harrison
Music engraving and book layout by Simon and Jennie Troup of Digital Music Art
Fact files written and edited by Abbie Thomas
Notes written by Roland Perrin
Proof reading and copy editing by Gemma Bull, Jono Harrison and Jennie Troup
Cover design by Philip Millard of Rather Nice Design
Cover photograph: © Nomad_Soul (Shutterstock)

AUDIO
Produced by Jono Harrison
Engineered by Jono Harrison, Gary Sanctuary, Tim Bennett-Hart, Pete Riley, Richard Brook, Rory Harvey and Andy Robertson
Assisted by Paul Pritchard at Abbey Road
Recorded at Dock Street Studios, The Dairy and Abbey Road
Mixed by Patrick Phillips
Mastered by Francis Gorini

Supporting Tests recorded by Chris Stanbury and Jono Harrison

MUSICIANS
Piano and Keyboards: Jono Harrison, Gary Sanctuary, Ross Stanley & Tania Ilyashova
Drums & Percussion: Pete Riley and Richard Brook
Bass & Synth Bass: Andy Robertson
Guitars: Rory Harvey, Nat Martin and Jono Harrison
Saxophone: Jonathan Griffiths
Trombone: Tom George White and Norton York
Trumpet: Nick Mead and John Simpson
Lead and Backing Vocals: Glen Harvey & Katie Hector
Additional Programming: Jono Harrison

DISTRIBUTION
Exclusive Distributors: Hal Leonard

CONTACTING ROCKSCHOOL
www.rslawards.com
Telephone: +44 (0)345 460 4747
Email: *info@rslawards.com*

EXECUTIVE PRODUCERS
John Simpson, Norton York

Table of Contents

Welcome to Rockschool Piano Level/Grade 5

Welcome to Rockschool's Piano syllabus 2019. This syllabus is designed to support pianists in their progression from Debut to Level/Grade 8, through an engaging and rigorous pathway covering all the genres, stylistic elements, techniques and musical skills required for success as a contemporary pianist.

Piano Assessments

At each level/grade you have the option of taking one of two different types of assessment:

- Level/**Grade Assessment**
  A Level/Grade Assessment is a mixture of music performances, technical work and tests. You are required to prepare three pieces (two of which may be Free Choice Pieces) and the contents of the Technical Exercise section. This accounts for 75% of the assessment marks. The other 25% consists of: either a Sight Reading or an Improvisation & Interpretation test (10%), two Ear Tests (10%), and finally you will be asked five General Musicianship Questions (5%). The pass mark is 60%.

- **Performance Certificate**
  A Performance Certificate is equivalent to a Level/Grade Assessment, but in a Performance Certificate you are required to perform five pieces. A maximum of three of these can be Free Choice Pieces. Each song is marked out of 20 and the pass mark is 60%.

All elements required to participate in a Rockschool assessment can be found in the level/grade book. These are as follows:

- **Assessment Pieces**
  The 2019 syllabus comprises six 'hit tune' arrangements, benchmarked and devised so as to equip contemporary pianists with industry-relevant skills in any performance environment. These fall into three categories:

  Melody & Accompaniment
  These arrangements are performed to full band backing tracks, with the piano performing both melody and accompaniment

  Solo Piano Arrangement
  These are full solo piano arrangements, performed without backing tracks

  Vocal Accompaniment
  These arrangements cover the skills required of contemporary pianists in ensemble environments, be they on the stage or in the studio. The backing tracks feature vocalists, and the piano parts are reflective of what session pianists would perform live or on mainstream commercial recordings

  Each 'hit tune' arrangement is preceded by a Fact File, giving surrounding context to the piece and the original performers/recording artists.

  Furthermore, at the end of each arrangement you will find notes giving additional supportive context to get the most out of the pieces.

- **Technical Exercises**
  There are either three or four groups of technical exercise, depending on the level/grade:

  Debut–Level/Grade 8:
  Group A: Scales
  Group B: Arpeggios/Broken Chords
  Group C: Chord Voicings

  Levels/Grades 4–8 only:
  Group D: Technical Study

- **Supporting Tests**
  There are three types of unprepared supporting tests in the assessment:

1. The first type can be one of two options (this is the *candidate's* choice):

   Either:
   Sight Reading tests, developing the musician's ability to read and perform previously unseen material;

   or:
   Improvisation & Interpretation tests, developing the musician's ability to develop previously unseen material in a stylistic way and perform improvised passages of melody. The book contains examples of both types of test – equivalent 'unseen' examples will be provided for the assessment

2. **Ear Tests**
   Debut–Level/Grade 3: feature Melodic Recall and Chord Recognition
   Levels/Grades 4–8: feature Melodic Recall and Harmonic Recall

3. **General Musicianship Questions (GMQs)**, which you will be asked by the assessor at the end of each assessment

General Information

You will find information on assessment procedures, including online assessment entry, marking schemes, information on Free Choice Pieces and improvisation requirements for each level/grade.

Audio

In addition to the level/grade book, we have also provided audio in the form of backing tracks (minus piano) and full tracks (including piano) for all 'hit tune' arrangements, technical exercises and supporting tests (where applicable). We have provided professional performance recordings of all solo piano pieces in the syllabus. This audio can be downloaded from RSL directly at *www.rslawards.com/downloads*

You will need to input this code when prompted: **3HFXB248RZ**

The audio files are supplied in MP3 format. Once downloaded you will be able to play them on any compatible device.

Further Information

You can find further details about Rockschool's Contemporary Piano syllabus by downloading the syllabus guide from our website: *www.rslawards.com*

All candidates should download and read the accompanying syllabus guide when using this level/grade book.

Performance and Technical Guidance

Fingering
Any fingering annotation is given as a guide only.

Interpretation
Notation should be performed exactly as written, except where there are performance indications to ad. lib, improvise, develop, etc. In these instances, the candidate will be marked on their ability to interpret the music in a stylistically appropriate way, commensurate with the level.

Adaptation
A small degree of adaptation is allowed where, for example, hand stretches do not facilitate the required notated parts. Marks may be deducted if adaptation results in over-simplification of the notation. If in doubt you can submit any adaptation enquiries to *info@rslawards.com*

Articulation & Dynamics
Where articulation and dynamics are marked on the notation, they should be followed. Where it is open to interpretation, the candidate is free to take their own approach.

Pedalling
The candidate may use the pedal freely at any level/grade, but it should be applied judiciously as marks may be deducted for any over usage resulting in an unclear tone. In addition, where pedalling is written into (or out of) the notation, this should be observed.

Chord Symbols
Most hit tune arrangements have chord symbols written above the notation. This is purely for guidance, and to assist the candidate and teacher.

A Thousand Miles

SONG TITLE: 'A THOUSAND MILES'
ALBUM: BE NOT NOBODY
RELEASED: 2002
LABEL: A&M
GENRE: BAROQUE POP/POP ROCK
WRITTEN BY: VANESSA CARLTON
PRODUCED BY: RON FAIR/
CURTIS SCHWEITZER
US CHART PEAK: 5

'A Thousand Miles' was a hit for American singer songwriter, Vanessa Carlton. The song was released as the lead single for Carlton's debut studio album, *Be Not Nobody*, and became her breakthrough to commercial success. The track achieved global success, reaching the top ten in the UK singles charts and topping the Australian chart. Carlton also had success with the hit in France, Italy, The Netherlands and Ireland.

Vanessa Carlton began writing the hit at her parent's house in Philadelphia in the summer of 1998, starting with the unforgettable piano riff which famously introduces the song. Meeting a writer's block along the way, she found the determination to finish it a few months later after receiving positive feedback on playing it to a record producer. On finishing the song she named it 'Interlude', a name that many would suggest she change and of course eventually became 'A Thousand Miles'.

Carlton worked hard for success, sending demos to producers and labels whenever she could and standing firm when offers were made which she felt would jeopardise her sound. Some years down the line, having sent out countless demos and turned down several offers, one of Carlton's tapes had found its way to head of A&M Records, Ron Fair. Fair loved the demo and was keen to work with Carlton, but felt that some of the music was a little disjointed and lacked the emotional pull it should be feeling. Although Carlton had turned down many offers from producers and labels in the past, due to their demands for change, she seemed to take Fair's advice on board and the two worked together to create something brilliant. Many changes were made to the original demo of this song, including the change of name, a shortened piano intro and an orchestral section. It would seem that Fair was indeed right to make these decisions as 'A Thousand Miles' soon became a household name and it's popularity was spreading worldwide.

'A Thousand Miles' received three Grammy award nominations, for Record of the Year, Song of the Year and Best Instrumental Arrangement Accompanying Vocalist(s). Sadly, these remained only nominations and she lost out on all three, with Norah Jones taking Record of the Year for 'Don't Know Why'. The song proved extremely popular with US troops at the time of its release and quickly became the most requested song on radio station 'British Forces Broadcasting Service'.

A Thousand Miles

Vanessa Carlton

Words & Music by Vanessa Carlton

B5/E F♯add4 B/D♯ E B5/E F♯add4 B/D♯ E
mp
mf
[9]
B5/E F♯add4 B/D♯ B/E B5/E F♯add4 B/D♯ B/E
[11]
B
Esus2 B/F♯ Badd9/D♯ Esus2 B/F♯ Badd9/D♯
mp
[13]
Esus2 B/F♯ Badd9/D♯ Esus2 F♯
[15]
C
Esus2 F♯add4 B/D♯ E
mf
[17]

Esus2 F♯add4 B/D♯ E Esus2 F♯add4
[19]
B/D♯ E G♯m7 F♯6/A♯ F♯
[22]
Esus2 F♯add4 B/D♯ E Esus2 F♯add4 B/D♯ E
[25]
Esus2 F♯add4 B/D♯ E Esus2 F♯add4 B/D♯ E6
[27]
D
G♯m7 F♯/A♯ Bmaj7 F♯/C♯ G♯m7 F♯/A♯
mp
[29]
8vb

Bmaj7 F♯/C♯ G♯m7 F♯/A♯
[32]
(8vb)
Bmaj7 F♯/C♯ G♯m7 F♯/A♯ F♯7sus4
f
subito p
[34]
(8vb)
E
B5/E F♯add4 B/D♯ E B5/E F♯add4 B/D♯ E
mf
[37]
B5/E F♯add4 B/D♯ B/E B5/E F♯add4 B/D♯ B/E
[39]
B5/E F♯add4 B/D♯ B/E B5/E F♯add4 B/D♯ B/E
mf
[41]

B5/E F♯add4 B/D♯ B/E B5/E F♯add4 B/D♯ B/E
f
[43]
F
Esus2 B/F♯ Badd9/D♯ Esus2 B/F♯ Badd9/D♯
mp
[45]
Esus2 B/F♯ Badd9/D♯ Esus2 F♯
[47]
G
Esus2 F♯add4 B/D♯ E
p
[50]
Esus2 F♯add4 B/D♯ E
[54]

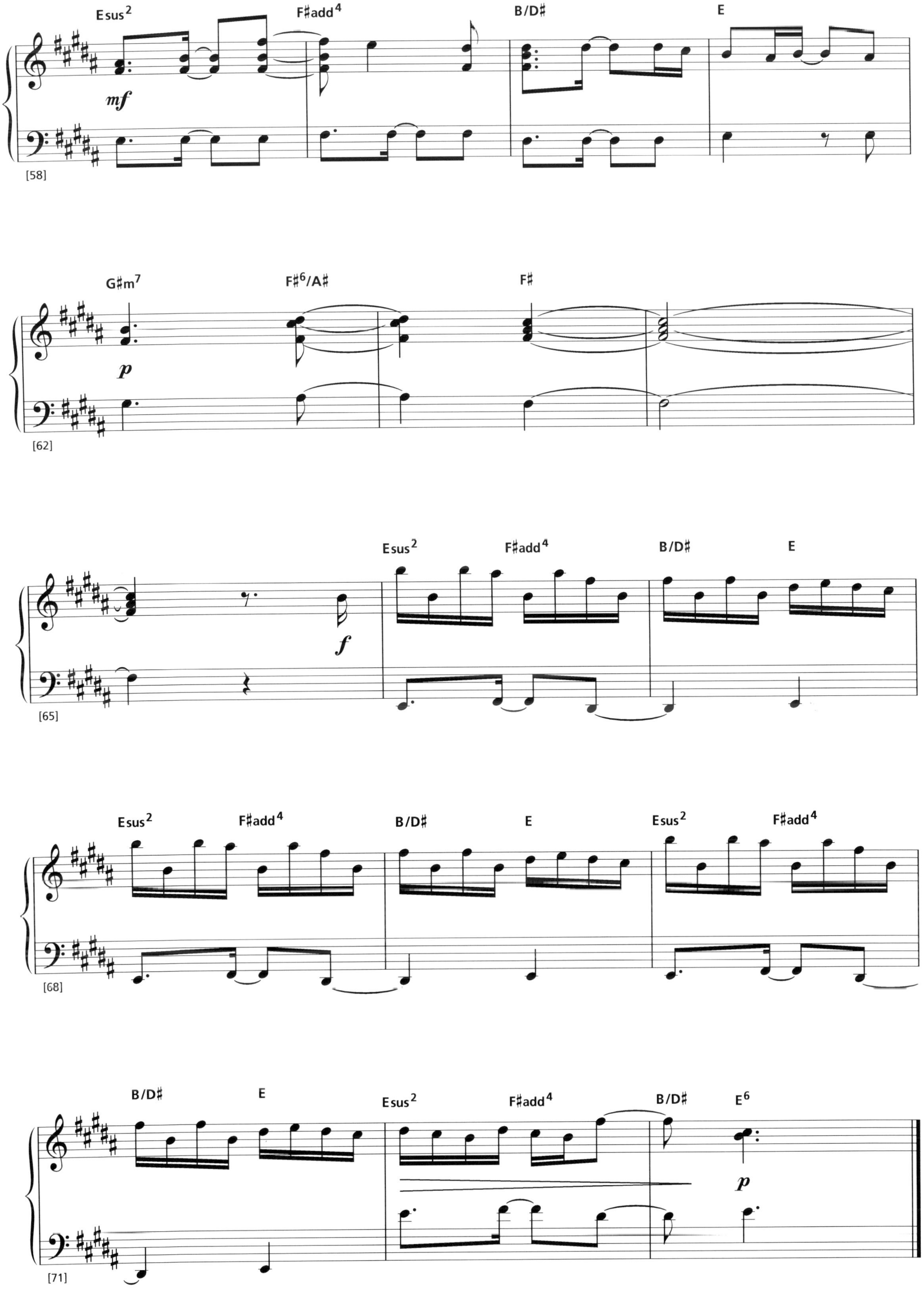
Esus2
F♯add4
B/D♯
E
mf
[58]
G♯m7
F♯6/A♯
F♯
p
[62]
Esus2
F♯add4
B/D♯
E
f
[65]
Esus2
F♯add4
B/D♯
E
Esus2
F♯add4
[68]
B/D♯
E
Esus2
F♯add4
B/D♯
E6
p
[71]

Notes

This song is full of subtle light and shade with quick transitions between melodic and rhythmic ideas. It is important for the performer to observe the dynamics carefully as this detail helps to shape and emphasise the shifting, restless feel of the song.

The 16th-note phrase found in the opening four measures of the right-hand part is re-visited throughout the song with slight variations. Students should take time to master this pattern in isolation from the left hand part and at a slower tempo. Once secure, students should read through the whole arrangement to see where this pattern is repeated, identifying and comparing the differences. Once secure, these passages should sound light and effortless with a precise delivery.

Measures 5 and 6 should be *legato* and without any hint of accent or *staccato*. Both hands should be equally balanced with the rhythmic pattern carefully observed.

This light and precise approach also applies to section B. As the left and right hand parts alternate in measures 13 to 15, care should be taken to observe the rests between each phrase, keeping the 16th notes short and un-accented.

The opening six measures of section C builds on the original syncopated groove with both hands repeating the two-beat pattern. Care should be taken to keep a steady quarter-note pulse and to avoid the music inadvertently speeding up. Although the volume is *mezzo forte* at this point, students need to be careful to balance parts appropriately to allow the melody line to be clearly heard above the accompaniment.

Section D creates a sudden contrast with the previous section with both a drop in register and volume. Keeping the parts well balanced and *legato*, take care not to anticipate the *crescendo* too early. The *subito piano* in measure 36 followed by an immediate shift again back to *mezzo forte* is a key moment in the song. Students should take time carefully rehearsing this section with particular attention to these dynamic changes, keeping a steady pulse throughout.

While section F is an almost direct repeat of the previous section B, section G is a pared down version of C and should be played *piano*. Maintaining this volume throughout the section will allow the performer dynamic space to create a contrasting final flourish as the 16th-note melody returns for a final time at *forte*.

Teardrop

SONG TITLE: 'TEARDROP'
ALBUM: MEZZANINE
RELEASED: 1998
LABEL: VIRGIN
GENRE: TRIP HOP/ELECTRONICA
WRITTEN BY: ROBERT DEL NAJA/ ELIZABETH FRASER/ GRANTLEY MARSHALL/ ANDREW VOWLES
PRODUCED BY: NEIL DAVIDGE/ MASSIVE ATTACK
US CHART PEAK: N/A

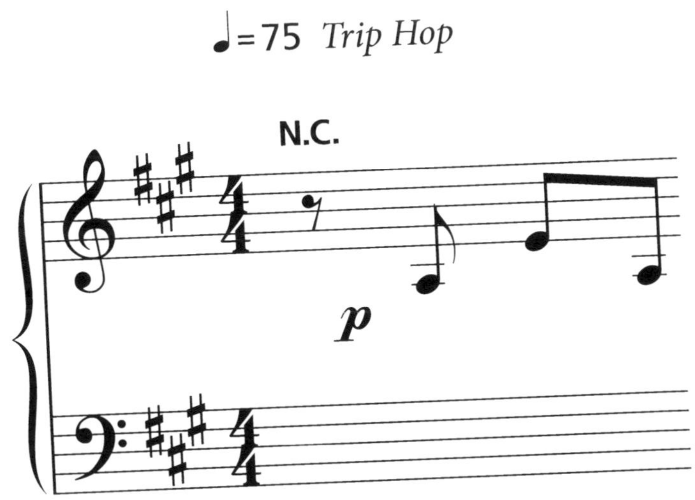

'Teardrop' was a top ten hit for British trip hop (a fusion of hip hop and electronica) group, Massive Attack. The song features on their third studio album, *Mezzanine* (1998), and was the second song to be released from said album. *Mezzanine* topped the album charts in the UK, Australia, Ireland and New Zealand, making it the groups most commercially successful release to date. Their fourth studio album, 100th Window, also topped the UK album chart in 2003.

'Teardrop' was written by the three founding members of Massive Attack (Robert Del Naja, Grantley Marshall and Andrew Vowles), as well as guest vocalist Elizabeth Fraser (Cocteau Twins). The idea for the song originally stemmed from a simple harpsichord riff and grew to become something quite unique in sound. Looking for a guest vocalist, Andrew Vowles sent the demo to Madonna, hoping she would perform the vocal as she had done for their earlier collaboration on 'I Want You'. Unfortunately, Vowles was outvoted by fellow bandmates Marshall and Del Naja and to Madonna's dismay the band didn't choose her for guest vocals. Instead, Elizabeth Fraser of Cocteau Twins was brought in and the result did not disappoint. Fraser delivers a haunting and emotional lyrical performance, one which she claims was inspired by the untimely passing of her dear friend Jeff Buckley.

'Teardrop' peaked at number 10 in the UK singles chart and remains their only top ten hit to date. The song has featured heavily in television and film broadcasts, including US hit series' Prison Break and House.

The song has proved a popular cover choice amongst musicians, with many having released their reworkings over the years. Newton Faulkner's 2007 version features a complex acoustic guitar accompaniment, which features in our 2016 Acoustic Guitar syllabus, and made it to number 60 in the UK singles chart. British band Elbow performed 'Teardrop' for a BBC Radio 1 Live Lounge session in 2003 and their version proved so popular that they decided to include a studio version on their 'Not a Job' single the following year. Last but by no means least, O'Hooley & Tidow were praised for their intricate adaptation of the track with Guardian music critic Jude Rogers voting it one of the best tracks of 2012.

Massive attack have been praised for their original and exclusive sound and were awarded the 'Innovation in Sound Award' by Q magazine in 2008. The group have proved particularly successful in Europe and have won several awards reflecting this, including the MTV Europe Music Award for Best Video with 'Teardrop' and the award for Best Foreign Album for *Mezzanine* at the 1998 Fryderyk awards (Poland).

Teardrop

Massive Attack

Asus4
Asus4/G
[13]
Dsus2
3
Asus4
[15]
Fmaj7
G
3
[17]
A
Asus4
[19]
Asus4
Asus4/G
mf
[21]

Dsus2/4
Asus4
[23]
Asus4
Asus4/G
[25]
Dsus4
Asus4
[27]
Fmaj7
G
[29]
A
Fmaj7
[31]
G
Fmaj7
[33]

G
A
Fmaj7
f
[35]
G
Fmaj7
mp
[38]
Gsus2
Asus4
p
[41]
F6/9
G6/9
A
3
[44]
F6/9
G6/9
Asus4
[47]
Asus4
[50]

Notes

'Teardrop' is a laid back song with an underlying forward driving groove, creating a relaxed yet brooding drama. Space, relaxation and an insistent groove are the fundamentals of the style.

Before beginning to play the opening eight measures, students should look to measure 9 and internalise the opening melodic phrase. This will help establish a secure tempo.

At measure 9, the arrangement has a three-part texture. Here, the melody should be projected clearly, while the inner harmony parts should be kept quieter and *legato*. In the lowest voice, the bass part should be a little quieter than the melody, but still provide a sense of solidity.

There is a further challenge in the variety of rhythms contained in the melody, in particular switching from 16th-note subdivisions to eighth-note triplets. Working to a metronome click or counting out loud, students should isolate the more challenging rhythmic passages and practise at a slower tempo until secure.

In measures 21 to 37, the performer will need to employ careful use of the pedal to sustain the whole notes while moving the hand position to play the eighth-note pattern in beats two to four. Students should practise the right-hand spread chord in measure 38 to get an effortless sounding and even spread of notes downwards.

The tied chord should be held over into measure 41 for its full length before carefully continuing to count through measure 42. A re-introduction of the motif (measures 43–45) sets up a piano outro (measure 46 to end), which features some melodic ideas drawn from the motif and the vocal melody. Although at a *piano* dynamic, these can still be played with expression and shape.

Throughout the piece, pedalling can be applied not just for *legato* purposes, but for tone. This is an important aspect of the technique, where light touches at certain points can bring extra sonority to the music as the overtones of the strings resonate. It may be useful to experiment with this in mind, exploiting the contrast between pedalled and non-pedalled passages.

Every Little Thing She Does Is Magic

SONG TITLE: 'EVERY LITTLE THING SHE DOES IS MAGIC'
ALBUM: GHOST IN THE MACHINE
RELEASED: 1981
LABEL: A&M
WRITTEN BY: STING
PRODUCED BY: HUGH PADGHAM/ STEWART COPELAND/ STING/ANDY SUMMERS
US CHART PEAK: 3

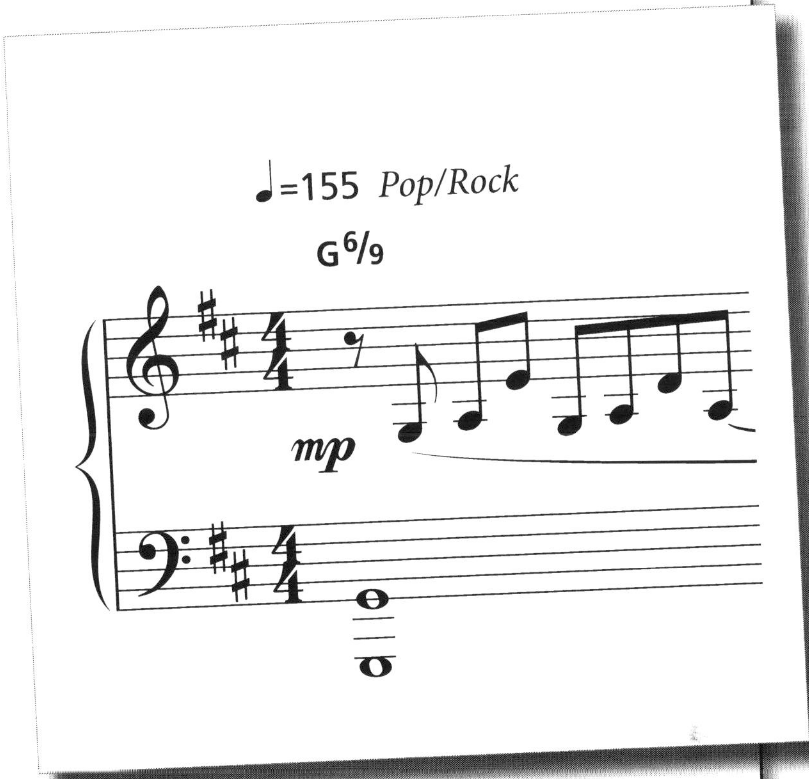

'Every Little Thing She Does Is Magic' was a global hit for British rock band The Police, taken from their fourth studio album *Ghost in The Machine.* The track was officially released in the November of 1981, but singer/bassist Sting actually wrote the hit several years before this during a songwriting session in 1976. The song could be described as a little 'lighter' than the sound usually associated with The Police, and on looking into this further it's clear that there is a fascinating story behind the creation of the song.

When Sting initially wrote the song in 1976 he recorded a simple demo to present to the rest of the band. It was met with low regard by both Andy Summers (guitar) and Stewart Copeland (drums) who both felt that it wasn't the right genre for them, but Sting persevered and brought in a session pianist (Jean Roussel) to perform on the official recording of the track. Summers and Copeland were uneasy with the addition of piano, but they left the decision in Sting's capable hands and the end result did not disappoint. It's said that Roussel recorded as many as 12 piano tracks for the hit and the outcome was remarkable. Suddenly a band who had never previously used piano on a recording had released a piano lead hit.

'Every Little Thing She Does Is Magic' has an incredibly unique sound, with the vocals set back from the music, another aspect of the song which leads to an interesting story. Having presented the band with his original demo, Sting found that they were struggling to recreate the right sound in the studio. After many hours of torment and hundreds of disregarded takes the band went on to make an unusual and brave decision – they recorded over the top of the original demo. Many believe this is how they created such a unique and recognisable sound for the song, with Sting's demo vocal remaining on the official track.

Although the song was originally met with concern from his fellow band members, Sting's instinct was absolutely correct and 'Every Little Thing She Does Is Magic' went on to become a worldwide success, topping the singles chart in 6 countries and making the top 20 in many more. Although The Police weren't widely known for their use of a piano, in this instance the decision was inspired and the result was a fantastically rewarding track to both listen to and to play.

Every Little Thing She Does Is Magic

The Police

B
A
A/C♯
D
[25]
To Coda
A
A/C♯
D
B♭
C/F
[29]
G6/9
A7sus4
G6/9/B
D/C♯
mp
[34]
C
G6/9
A7sus4
G6/9/B
D/C♯
[38]
Dsus4
D
[42]
[46]

G A D G A D G A D
D.𝄋. al Coda 𝄌
f
[50]
𝄌 Coda
A B♭
D
C/F Gm7 Am7
mf
[54]
B♭maj7 C/F D
[58]
B♭ C/F Gm7 Am7
[62]
Gm7 C/F D G A D
[66]
G A B♭ C/F Gm7 Am7 B♭maj7
[70]

C/F
D
[75]
E
B♭
C/F
Gm7
Am7
B♭maj7
8va
[79]
C/F
D
f
[83]
B♭maj7
C6/F
[87]
Gm9
Am11
B♭maj7♯11
C/F
[91]
Dsus4
mp
p
8vb
[95]

Notes

The main feeling students need to capture in this arrangement is one of exuberance, reflected in the fast tempo and frequent use of eighth-note passages.

Students would benefit from listening to the original recording to gain an understanding of how this piano arrangement is a combination of both the instrument parts and the original vocal melody. This will help to phrase, shape and balance the parts within the two hands.

The *crescendo* that begins in measure 21 is important in building the music up to the next section. Students should aim for a smooth and steady increase of volume from *mezzo piano* to *forte* with an accented emphasis on the final eighth note of measure 23. Note that this note is also articulated with a *staccato* in both hands to enhance the punchy ending. After observing two beats of silence, the energy should immediate pick right back up to drive the music forward into the upbeat chorus at letter B. Students should take care to observe the eighth-note rest on beat 4 in the right hand melody in measures 25, 27 and 29.

Letter C features the same opening melody with a new arrangement. Students are required to make a clear difference between the melodic line and left hand accompaniment. The busy left hand part needs to be quieter than the right hand part, staying even and flowing. Students should practise the hand position shift from the end of measure 41 into 42 and again from the end of measure 45 into 46 to make sure that they are prepared to move the left hand position down in time for the start of the following pattern beginning on a low G to avoid arriving late.

Section D features longer sustained and syncopated chords. It is important that the performer keeps a clear pulse throughout this section to keep the momentum of the music and tempo steady. Note the descending glissando in measure 82. This needs to be carefully timed so that the performer is ready to play the next musical phrase in measure 83, the effect sounding effortless. Students may benefit from the playing the right hand part of measures 81 to 84 in isolation as a loop, counting out loud to master the timing and hand position moves.

The coda has some beautiful contrasting and spacious music. Students should aim for a full, rich tone by ensuring that all the notes of every chord are fully sounded.

Dangerous

SONG TITLE: 'DANGEROUS'
ALBUM: LISTEN
RELEASED: 2014
LABEL: PARLOPHONE
GENRE: SYNTHPOP/HOUSE
WRITTEN BY: DAVID GUETTA/GIORGIO TUINFORT/SAM MARTIN/ JASON EVIGAN/ LINDY ROBBINS
PRODUCED BY: DAVID GUETTA/GIORGIO TUINFORT/SAM MARTIN/ JASON EVIGAN
US CHART PEAK: 56

'Dangerous' was the second single to be released from French music producer David Guetta's sixth studio album, *Listen.* The track features vocals by Grammy Award winning American singer-songwriter Sam Martin. 'Dangerous' peaked at number 5 in the UK official singles chart and number 2 on the UK dance singles chart, while only making it to number 56 on the US singles chart it did manage 6th place in the US dance chart. The song was well received globally and actually topped the charts in more than fifteen countries across Europe, including Luxembourg, Sweden, Poland, Slovakia, Spain and of course Guetta's native France.

The track was co-written by the two featuring artists, Guetta and Martin, with additional input from producer and songwriter Giorgio Tuinfort, singer-songwriter Jason Evigan and multi-platinum selling songwriter Lindy Robbins. The writing and production team for this song hold quite the track record between them, with the likes of Robbins having written hits for Jennifer Hudson, One Direction and Jason Derulo (to name a few). The track features guest acoustic drums from Ron Thaler, professionally known as Blondie Boy, who is well known for several session appearances including Alicia Key's double Grammy Award winning 'No One'. The recording is led heavily by a prominent rhythm section, paired with an impressive synth line which almost pays homage to the typical 1980s dance sound.

David Guetta has released seven studio albums over the years, with album sales of over nine million and single sales of over thirty million worldwide. His debut album, *Just a Little More Love,* was released in 2002 but it wasn't until his fourth studio album in 2009 that he achieved mainstream success. *One Love* includes hits 'When Love Takes Over', featuring vocals from Grammy Award winning singer Kelly Rowland, and 'Gettin' Over You' which topped the UK singles chart. Guetta is highly regarded in the world of dance music and is known for his successful collaborations. He holds nine Grammy nominations, with wins for Best Remixed Recording, Non-Classical with the aforementioned 'When Love Takes Over' in 2009 and Best Remixed Recording, Non-Classical with his hit 'Revolver' in 2010. Often referred to as the Grandfather of EDM, Guetta was an influential figure in the creation of Electronic Dance Music and remains innovative in the genre to this day.

Dangerous

David Guetta feat. Sam Martin

Words & Music by Lindy Robbins, Sam Martin, David Guetta, Giorgio Tuinfort & Jason Evigan

Em C Am D Em C
[15]
Am D Cmaj7 D
[18]
B
Em C Am D
[21]
Em C Am D C
[23]
D C D
[26]
C
Em C Am D
mp expressively, gradual cresc. on rpt.
[29]

Em
C
Am
D
[31]
Cmaj7
f
D
[33]
D
Em
C
Am
D
[35]
Em
C
Am
D
Em
C
[37]
Am
D
C
D
[40]
E
N.C.
pp
[43]

[45]
F
Em
C/E
Am/E
D
Em
C/E
mp
[47]
Am
D
C
D
mf
subito p
[50]
G
Em
C
Am
D
f
[54]
Em
C
Am
D
Em
C
[56]
Am
D
C
D
[59]

Notes

The rhythmic precision required to play this music convincingly will be helped if students lightly tap one foot on all four quarter notes in the measure, during practise, while keeping an inner feeling for the 16th-note subdivision of the beat.

The opening 16th-note pattern needs to be played rhythmically precisely with an even tone and secure *legato*. To help develop the finger strength and control required, a useful technical exercise would be to loop one measure of the 16th-note pattern and practise slowly, playing *staccato*. Starting at half speed, allow for a loose wrist, paying attention to the hand position and keeping the fingers gently rounded. Aim to keep the volume even across all notes to ensure that the traditionally weaker fourth and fifth fingers are matching the speed and volume of the other fingers. As the exercise is mastered, gradually increase the tempo. When the student returns to performing the passage at *legato*, it should controlled and even in tone.

The right-hand part in letters A and B, then later at D, are from the vocal melodies in the original recording and should sound above the lilting left-hand part. The challenge here is to play two simultaneous different articulations with a quieter more *legato* left hand part at the same time as a slightly more detached and forthright right-hand part. At section D, there the left hand should be punchier with quarter-note chords alternating with rapid spread chords.

The character of section F requires a keen observance of the rhythmic pattern and articulations to create space and texture. Note how there the right hand plays an accented note immediately after a *staccato* note in measures 47, 49 and 51. This should be practised in isolation to ensure the two articulations sound correctly. This section also requires careful observance of the varied dynamic indications.

The arpeggios in the left-hand part within section G require a loose wrist and good hand movement to reach up from the lowest note of each arpeggio to a fifth above and then stretch up to the tenth. This passage would benefit from playing the left hand separately and observing the wrist movement, first practising without the pedal to aim for precise timing and an even tone. Once secure, the performer can add careful pedalling and then introduce the right-hand part above.

SONG TITLE: LIFE ON MARS
ALBUM: HUNKY DORY
RELEASED: 1973
LABEL: RCA
GENRE: ROCK
VOCALS: DAVID BOWIE
PIANO: RICK WAKEMAN
GUITARS: MICK RONSON
BASS: TREVOR BOLDER
DRUMS: MICK WOODMANSEY
MELLOTRON & STRING ARRANGEMENT: MICK RONSON
WRITTEN BY: DAVID BOWIE
PRODUCED BY: KEN SCOTT
US CHART PEAK: N/A

The song was released in 1973 as a single from the 1971 album *Hunky Dory* (Bowie's fourth album) and stayed in the UK charts for thirteen weeks, peaking at No.3. The Daily Telegraph ranked the hit at the top of their 'Greatest Hits of All Time' list and in 2016 online music magazine Pitchfork titled it the best song of the 1970s. The track featured progressive rock band Yes' Rick Wakeman on guest piano.

The song was allegedly written as a parody of Frank Sinatra's 'My Way', with the liner notes of Bowie's song reading: 'inspired by Frankie'. Bowie has referred to the song as "my kind of modern take on 'My Way'"; although he often provides different explanations as to the song's meaning. He has been known to describe it as relationship: "you fall in love, you write a love song. This is a love song". Although he had previously said that is was about a young girl struggling with reality: "she's being told there's a far greater life somewhere and she's bitterly disappointed she doesn't have access to it".

Bowie himself said that he composed the song at the piano and "had the whole lyric and melody finished by late afternoon". Rick Wakeman embellished Bowie's original piano parts and Mick Ronson created a string arrangement that layered over this.

David Bowie has often been described as one of the most influential British rock stars due to his innovative ideas. He had an interest in embodying different personae (such as Ziggy Stardust) and the idea of telling cinematic stories. The selection of artists he gathered to play on this album and the producer, Ken Scott would all become part of the Ziggy Stardust and the Spiders from Mars phase. Bowie felt *Hunky Dory* was one of the most important albums in his career, stating: "It was like: I'm finding my feet. I'm starting to communicate what I want to do".

David Bowie sadly passed away on the 10th January 2016. A leading figure in the music industry, Bowie was regarded as one of the most influential musicians of the 20th century. His successes include an induction into the Rock and Roll Hall of Fame, eleven number 1 UK albums, five UK number 1 singles, five Grammy awards and four Ivor Novello awards. These accomplishments only scratch the surface of his career, but the list is simply too long to cover in full.

Life On Mars?

David Bowie

B♭
a tempo
E♭
Gm7
G♭aug
[13]
F
Fm
Cm7
E♭m7
[15]
B♭
E♭
Gm7
G♭aug
[17]
F
Fm
8va
Cm7
E♭m7
[19]
Gm
Gm/F♯
Gm7/F
Em7♭5
[21]
F
F♯dim
Gm
Ddim7
Am
B♭
B♭m
rall.
[23]

a tempo
F
F/E
F/E♭
D7
[27]
Gm
Gm/F
C7
[29]
F
F/E
F7/E♭
Dsus4
D7
[31]
Gm
Gm7/F
B♭/C
C
[33]
Cm/E♭
Caug/E
Fm
A♭/G♭
[35]
D♭
Faug/A
B♭m
Badd9♭5
poco rall.
[37]

B♭
a tempo
E♭
Gm7
G♭aug
[39]
F
Fm
Cm7
E♭m7
[41]
B♭
E♭
Gm7
G♭aug
[43]
F
Fm
Cm7
E♭m7
[45]
Gm
Gm/F♯
Gm7/F
Em7♭5
F
F♯dim
[47]
Gm
B♭/F
E♭
molto rall.
E♭m
B♭
[50]

Notes

This song requires a steady quarter-note pulse kept throughout and to carry the music across the syncopated rhythms.

Note that the chords in the right-hand part of measure 9 and, for some, in measure 10, involve a large hand stretch. If the student finds that this is physically not possible, they should simply omit the lowest note of these chords.

Students will notice that there are several places within the score that require accurate hand position changes, such as the chords in the right-hand part of measure 15 and again at measure 25. While these quarter-note chords are relatively slow moving, students should aim to move quickly between each chord position to allow each chord to sound for their full value. Students may find use of the pedal can be helpful at these points. Make sure to lift the pedal halfway through each of these measures, just before each chord change, to avoid a muddy texture.

Although the right hand should take the melodic lead for the majority of this song, while the left plays a supporting role, both hands should be evenly balanced in measures 29 and 30, as the melodic pattern passes back and forward between parts.

While the left hand poses fewer technical challenges than the right hand part, it is worth paying particular attention to the 16th-note descending chromatic figure repeated four times in measures 15 and 19, then again in measures 41 and 45. This faster octave work will benefit from playing slowly in isolation. Students should experiment with the finger pattern for this passage to establish what fits most comfortably under their fingers to produce an even and *legato* feel. While some might find using the first and fifth finger throughout works well, others might find it easier to use the fourth finger for the lower E flat.

You've Got A Friend In Me

SONG TITLE: 'YOU'VE GOT A FRIEND IN ME'
ALBUM: TOY STORY
RELEASED: 1996
LABEL: WALT DISNEY
GENRE: COUNTRY/POP
WRITTEN BY: RANDY NEWMAN
PRODUCED BY: RANDY NEWMAN
US CHART PEAK: N/A

'You've Got a Friend in Me' was written by Randy Newman, for use in the 1995 Disney classic Toy Story and later released as a single featuring Newman himself and Lyle Lovett. The song went on to appear in each Toy Story film in some capacity, either in its original format or song by one of the many endearing characters. Although the single didn't chart, the song itself was well received and was nominated for two prestigious awards; the Academy Award for Best Original Song and the Golden Globe for the same award, both of which it lost out on to Pocahontas' 'Colours of the Wind'.

Newman is an American singer-songwriter, arranger and composer. Since the 1980s he has been best known for his work in film scoring, especially for his work with Disney-Pixar for whom he has scored eight films. Although Newman's 'You've Got a Friend in Me' missed out on the above awards, many of his compositions for film were more successful in this sense and many of those were other Disney-Pixar collaborations. In 2002 he took the Academy Award for Best Original Song with his Monsters, Inc. classic 'If I Didn't Have You' and in 2011 he won the same coveted award with his song 'We Belong Together' written for Toy Story 3. Newman also holds seven Grammy Awards, including Best Song Written for a Motion Picture at the 2000 ceremony for 'When She Loved Me (from Toy Story 2) and the same award for his piece 'Our Town (from Cars) in 2006.

Disney-Pixar's Toy Story was the first feature-length film to be entirely computer-animated and was the first feature-length release from the highly regarded collaborating conglomerations. Toy Story was extremely well received, being nominated for three Academy Awards and winning a Special Achievement Academy Award for its contribution to animated film. Toy Story was followed by its sequel, Toy Story 2, in 1999 and its trilogy, Toy Story 3, in 2010. The franchise has been hugely successful and so far has grossed at over $1.9 billion worldwide. Disney-Pixar are currently working on Toy Story 4, expected for release in June 2019 we can rest assured that it will prove as popular as the previous films in the franchise.

You've Got A Friend In Me

Randy Newman

From 'Toy Story' (1995)

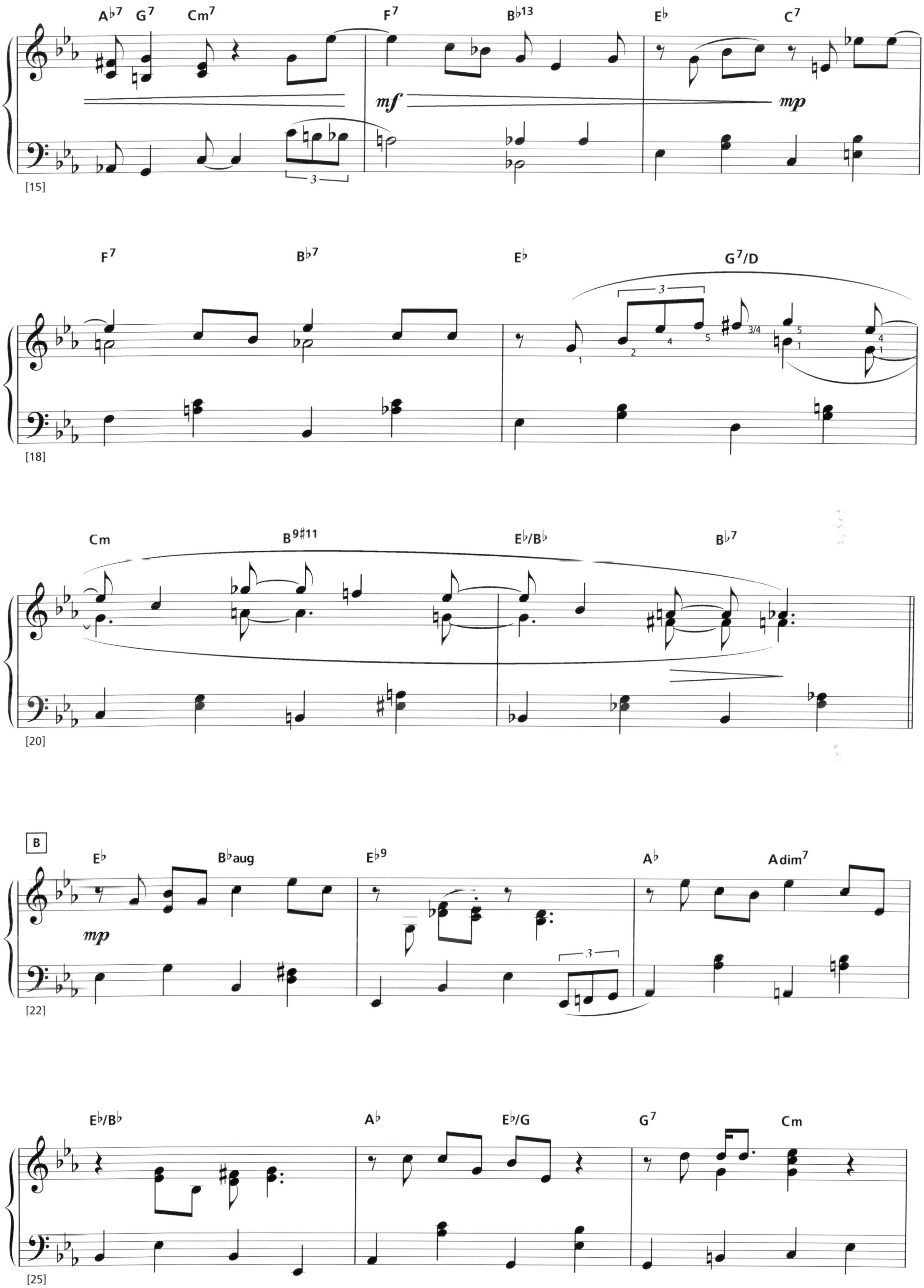
A♭7 G7 Cm7 F7 B♭13 E♭ C7
mf mp
[15]
F7 B♭7 E♭ G7/D
[18]
Cm B9♯11 E♭/B♭ B♭7
[20]
B
E♭ B♭aug E♭9 A♭ Adim7
mp
[22]
E♭/B♭ A♭ E♭/G G7 Cm
[25]

A♭ E♭/G G7 Cm A♭ E♭/G
[28]
G7 Cm F7 B♭13 E♭ C7
f
mp
[31]
F7 B♭13 E♭ E♭7
[34]
C
A♭ D7 E♭6 D7
mf
[36]
E♭6 D7 Em7 Fdim7 D/F♯
[39]

Gm
C7
Fm7
B♭13
[42]
D
E♭
B♭aug
E♭9
A♭
Adim7
mp
[44]
E♭/B♭
A♭
Adim7
rit.
E♭/B♭
G aug/B
Cm
f
[47]
a tempo
F7
B♭13
E♭
C7
F7
B♭13
p
[50]
E♭
C7
F7
B♭13
E♭
G7/D
mf
[53]
Cm
B9♯11
rit.
E♭/B♭
B♭7
E♭
p
[56]

Notes

This light-hearted tribute to friendship is heavily influenced by New Orleans piano styles. Students should be encouraged to listen to artists such as Jelly Roll Morton, Professor Longhair, Doctor John and the original performance of this song by Randy Newman for context.

Students need to be clear which parts in the right hand are the original vocal melody and which are accompaniment, to achieve the correct balance. It can be helpful to think of the piano part as representing a full band arrangement – for example, the left hand part (in keeping with the New Orleans style of the song) could be thought of as a tuba or a double bass. This will need to be controlled carefully to maintain clarity with the changes of dynamics through the piece. The notes do not sustain for very long, so they should bounce along – detached but not *staccato* – and any pedalling should be very light if being applied.

The swung rhythms of the music shouldn't be laboured – it can be a useful exercise to compare straight and swung eighth-note rhythms by tapping a foot on the pulse, and clapping the two subdivisions in order to understand the feel before playing the notes. Confidence with swung rhythms will help achieve the desired effect in performance.

An alternating fingering pattern is suggested at measure 36 (letter C) – this can be a useful technique on faster repeated notes to ensure that the delivery is smooth – this can also be adopted in measure 37. These are only suggestions for the ease of the performer and can be freely adapted.

Technical Exercises

In this section you will be required to play a selection of exercises drawn from each of the groups below. The assessor will be looking for the speed of your response and will also give credit for the level of your musicality. Please see the syllabus guide for details on the marking criteria.

- Candidates can choose to play ***either*** natural minor ***or*** harmonic minor scales
- Major scales, minor scales, chromatic scales and arpeggios need to be played hands together, in straight or swung feel, ascending and descending, across ***three*** octaves (except contrary motion scales, pentatonics, lydian and phrygian modes, which must be played over ***two*** octaves and extended arpeggios which are one octave only)
- Pentatonic scales are right hand only
- Lydian and Phrygian modes need to be played hands separately
- Groups A, B and C (scales, arpeggios and chords) need to be played from memory. You may use your book for Group D (technical studies)

Note that Groups A and B need to be played to a click and any fingerings shown are suggestions only.

Group A: Scales
The tempo for this group is ♩=126 bpm.

1. B major *(three octaves, two octave example shown)*

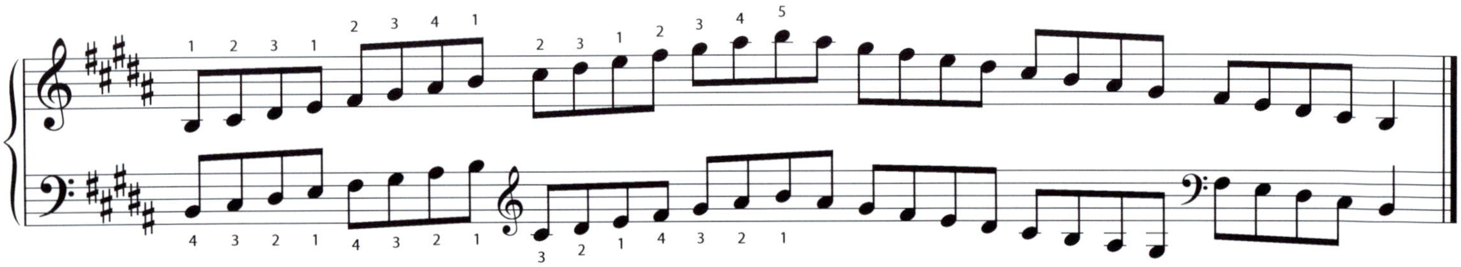

2. B major | contrary motion

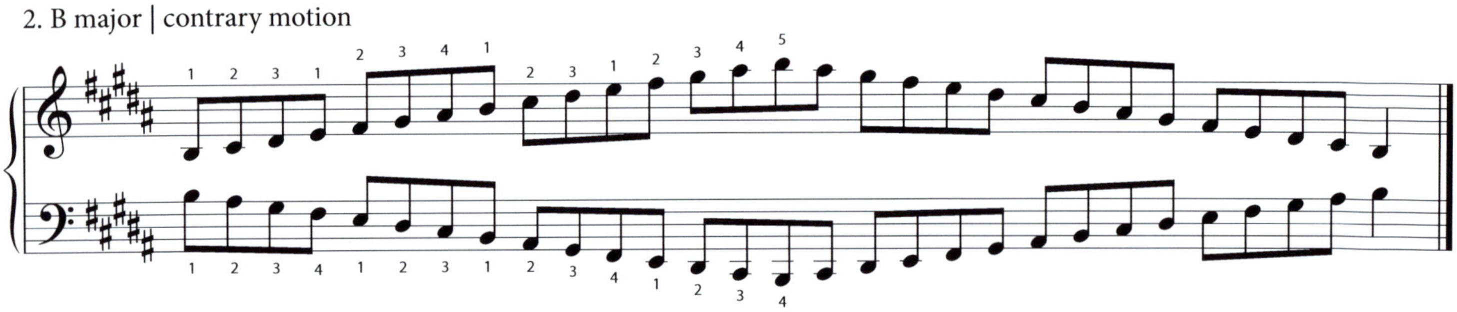

3. D♭ major *(three octaves, two octave example shown)*

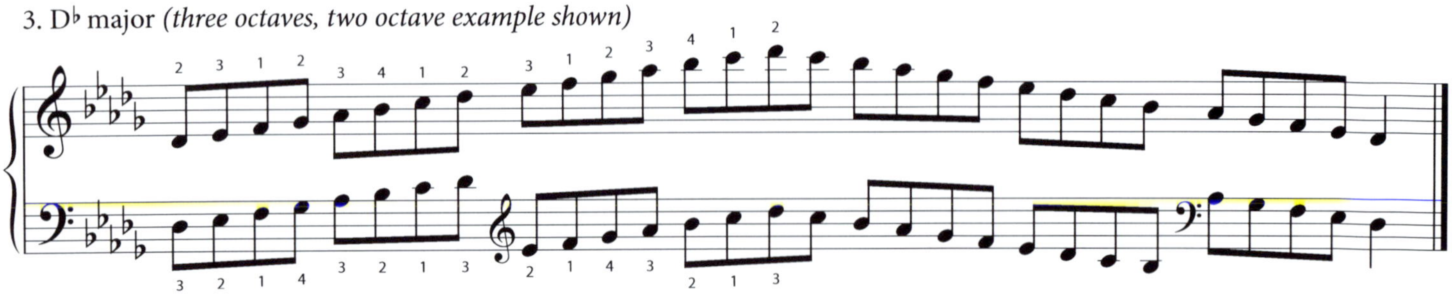

4. D♭ major | contrary motion

5. G♯ natural minor *(three octaves, two octave example shown)*

6. B♭ natural minor *(three octaves, two octave example shown)*

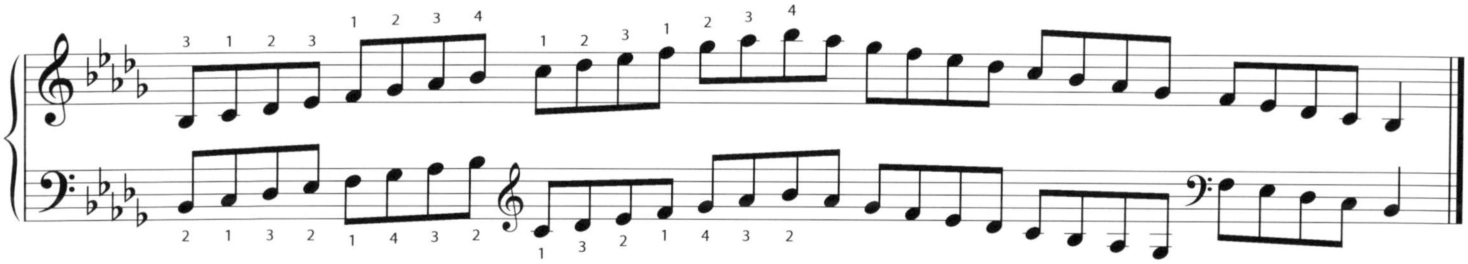

7. G♯ harmonic minor *(three octaves, two octave example shown)*

8. B♭ harmonic minor *(three octaves, two octave example shown)*

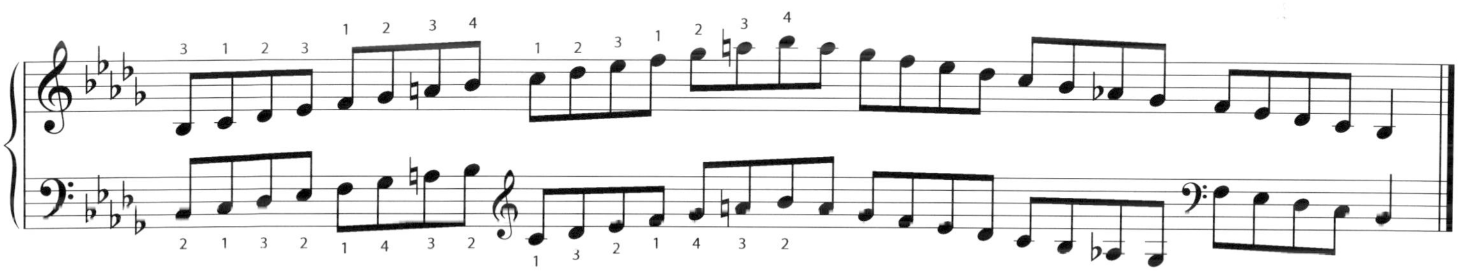

9. B major pentatonic | right hand

10. D♭ major pentatonic | right hand

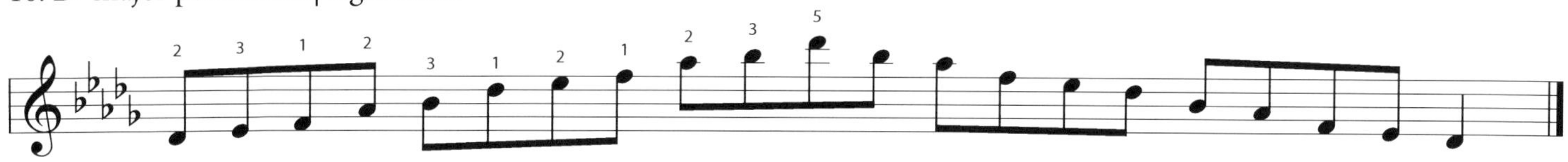

11. G♯ minor pentatonic | right hand

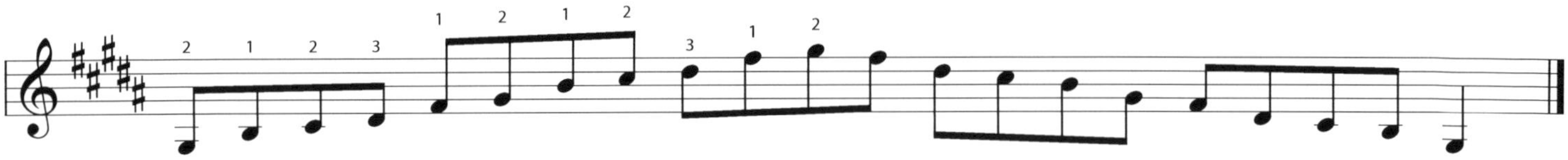

12. B♭ minor pentatonic | right hand

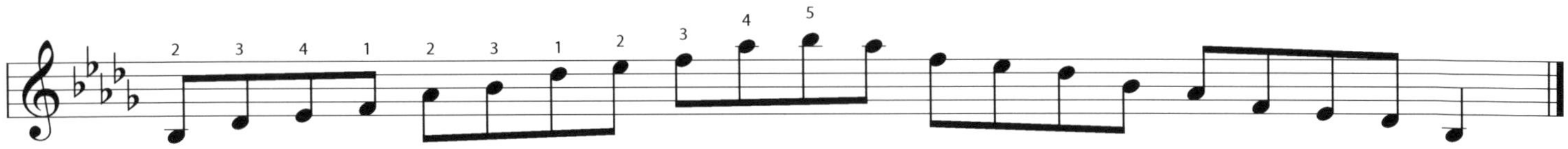

13. C lydian | right hand

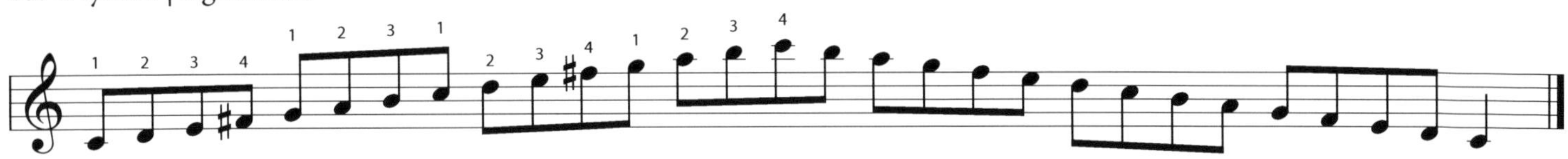

14. C lydian | left hand

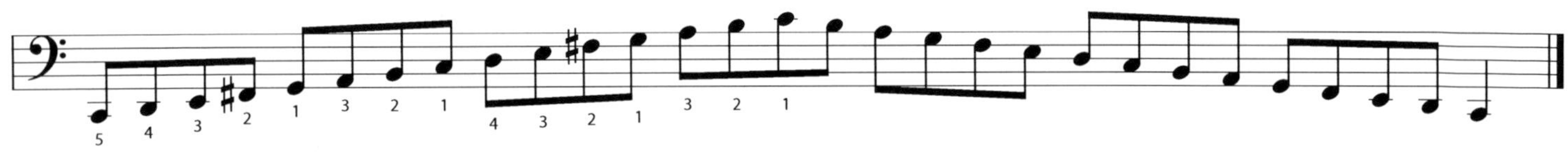

15. C phrygian | right hand

16. C phrygian | left hand

17. Chromatic Scale | starting on any white key chosen by the assessor, example given in B *(three octaves, two octave example shown)*

Group B: Arpeggios

The tempo for this group is ♩= 86 bpm.

1. B major arpeggio *(three octaves, two octave example shown)*

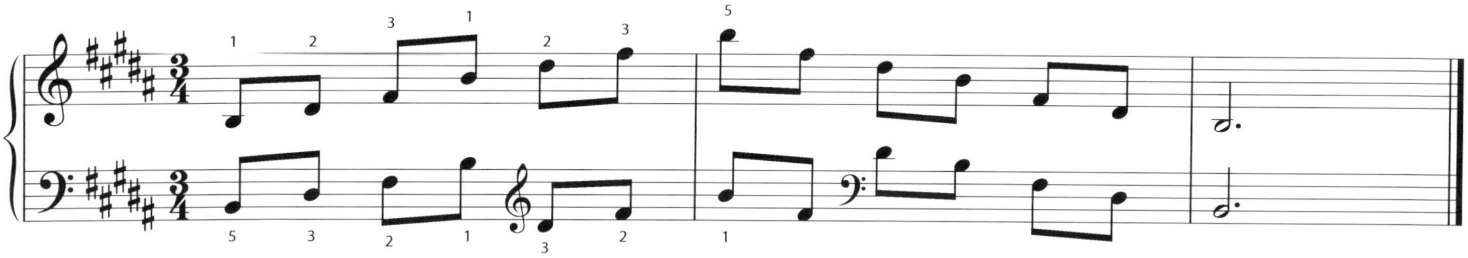

2. D♭ major arpeggio *(three octaves, two octave example shown)*

3. G♯ minor arpeggio *(three octaves, two octave example shown)*

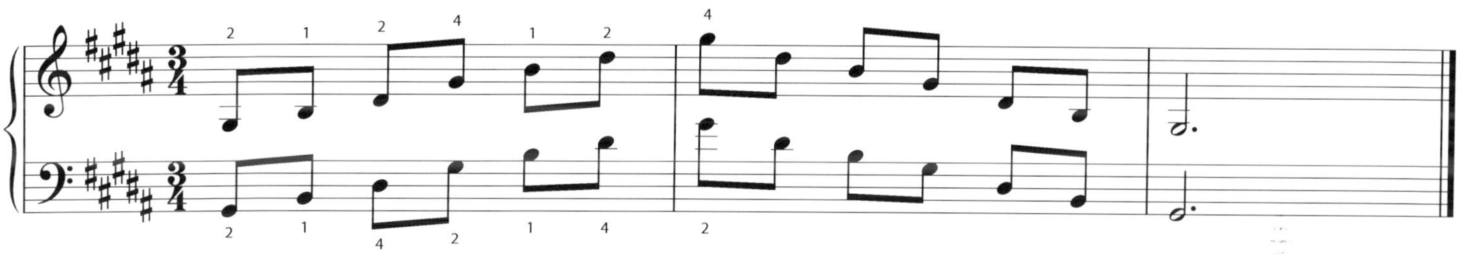

4. B♭ minor arpeggio *(three octaves, two octave example shown)*

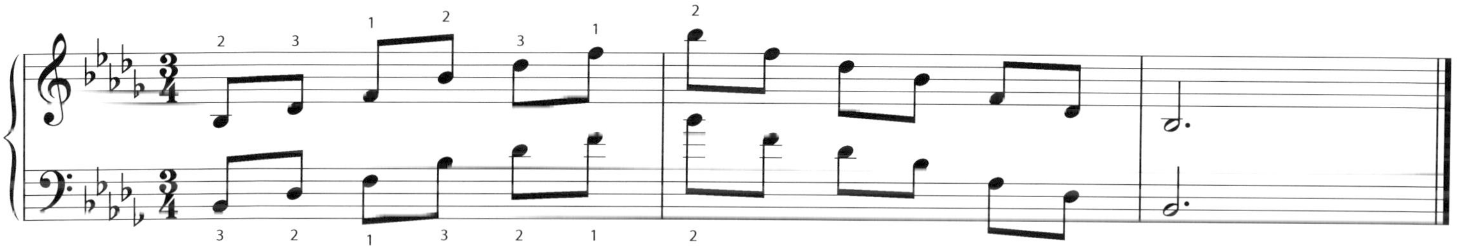

5. Cm maj^{7} arpeggio *(three octaves, two octave example shown)*

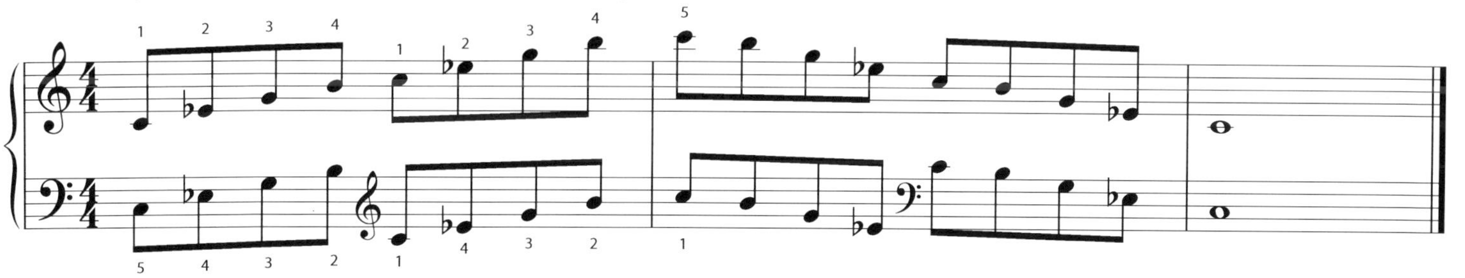

6. C^{7}add^4 arpeggio *(three octaves, two octave example shown)*

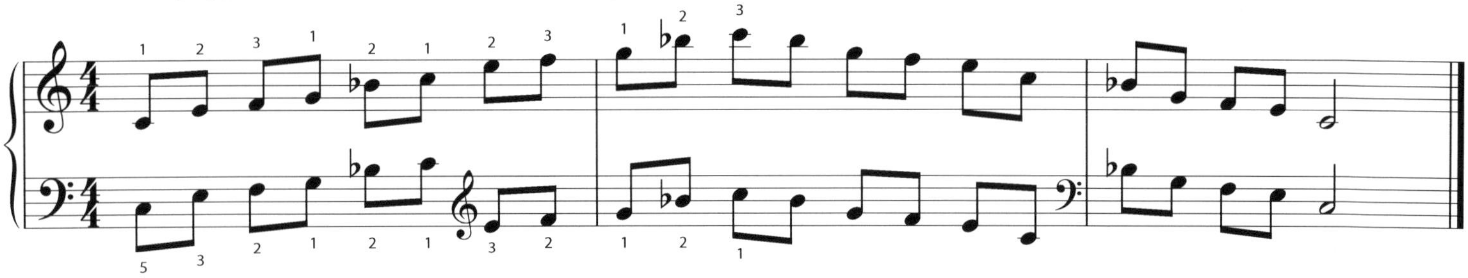

7. Cmaj$^{9\sharp 11}$ arpeggio | right hand

8. Cmaj$^{9\sharp 11}$ arpeggio | left hand

9. Cm^{11} arpeggio | right hand

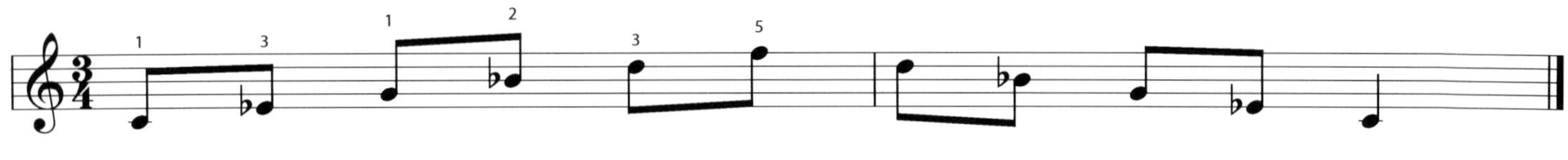

10. Cm^{11} arpeggio | left hand

Group C: Chord Voicings | Minor 11 and Major 9(♯11) Chords

In the assessment you will be asked to play one of the chord exercises below, from memory. The assessor will state the chord type. This test is performed in free time (without backing track or click), but the assessor will be looking for the speed of your response.

Ex 1: Cm11 chords

Ex 2: Cmaj9♯11 chords

Group D: Technical Studies

In the assessment you will be asked to perform your choice of one of the following three technical studies along with the accompanying backing track.

Example 1 | VIm – IIm – V – I progressions, syncopation and walking bass

Example 2 | Lydian modal study

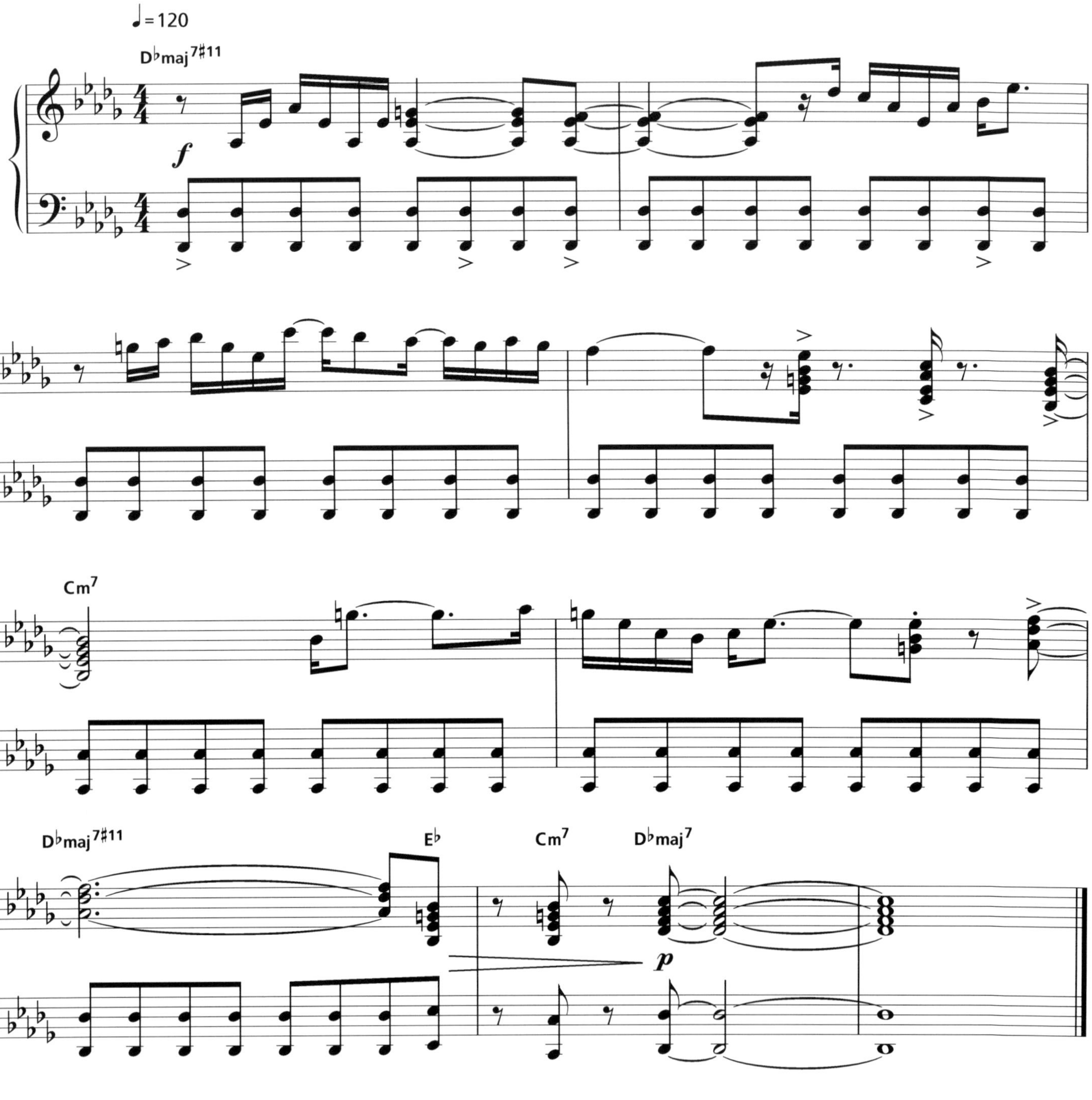

Example 3 | Phrygian modal study

Sight Reading

In the assessment, you have a choice between either a Sight Reading test or an Improvisation & Interpretation test. The assessor will ask you which one you wish to choose before commencing. Once you have decided you cannot change your mind.

In the sight reading test, the assessor will give you an 8–16 measure example in the key of either B major or D♭ major. You will first be given 90 seconds to practise, after which the assessor will play the backing track twice. The first time is for you to practise and the second time is for you to perform the final version for the assessment. For each playthrough, the backing track will begin with a one measure count-in. The tempo is ♩= 60–130.

During the practice time, you will be given the choice of a metronome click throughout or a one measure count in at the beginning.

The backing track is continuous, so once the first playthrough has finished, the count in of the second playing will start immediately.

Please note:

- You will be required to play all notation and create appropriate parts to chord symbols.
- Time signatures will be either 4/4 or 3/4.

Sight Reading | Example 1

Please note: The test shown is an example. The assessor will give you a different version in the assessment.

Sight Reading | Example 2

Please note: The test shown is an example. The assessor will give you a different version in the assessment.

Improvisation & Interpretation

In the assessment, you have a choice between either a Sight Reading test or an Improvisation & Interpretation test. The assessor will ask you which one you wish to choose before commencing. Once you have decided you cannot change your mind.

In the Improvisation & Interpretation test, the assessor will give you a 8–16 measure chord progression in the key of either B major or D♭ major. You will first be given 90 seconds to practise, after which the assessor will play the backing track twice. The first time is for you to practise and the second time is for you to perform the final version for the assessment. For each playthrough, the backing track will begin with a one measure count-in. The tempo is ♩=60–130.

During the practice time, you will be given the choice of a metronome click throughout or a one measure count-in at the beginning.

The backing track is continuous, so once the first playthrough has finished, the count-in of the second playing will start immediately.

You will need to improvise diatonic, single note melodies with right hand and chords in left hand.

Improvisation & Interpretation | Example 1

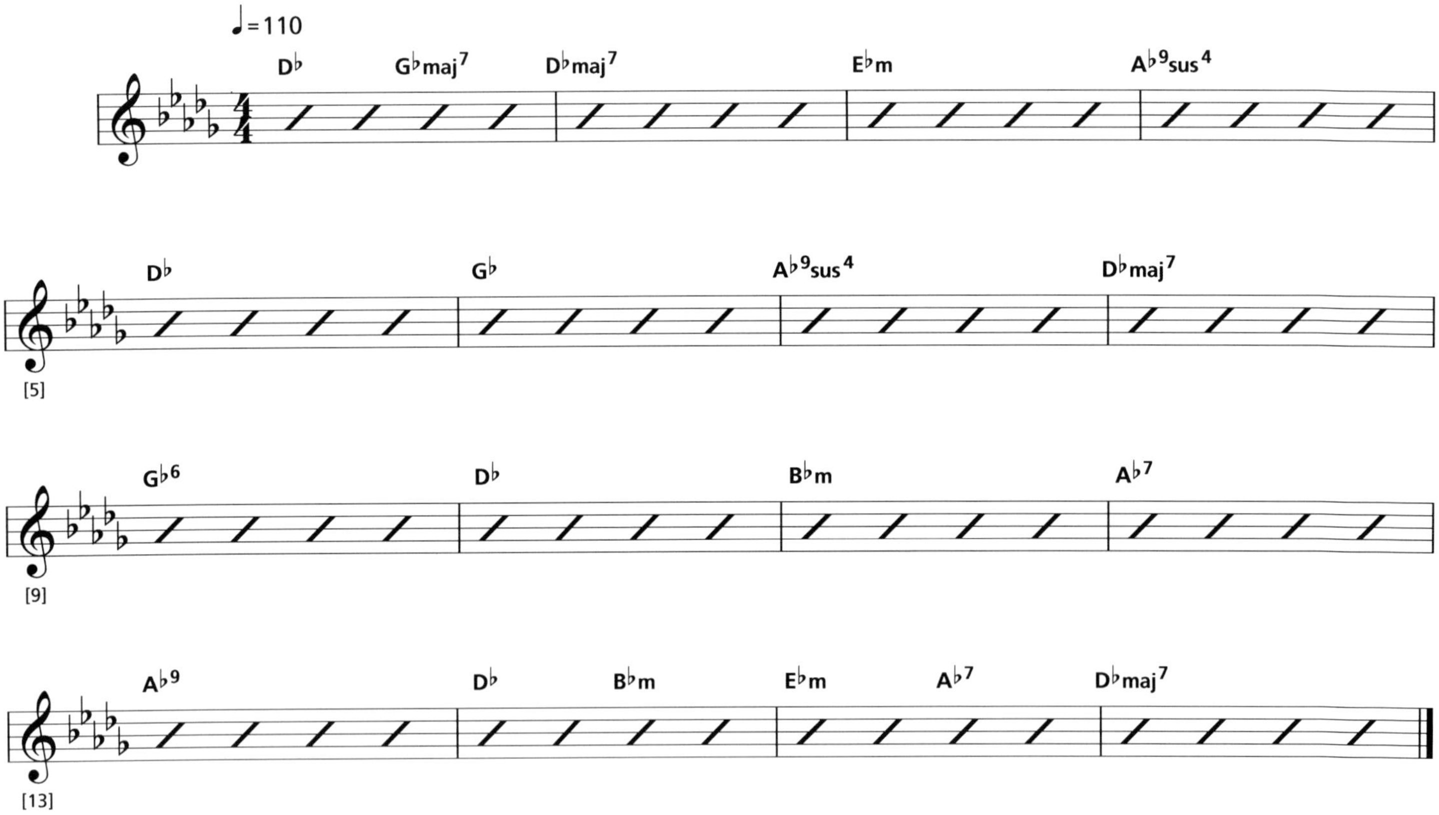

Please note: The test shown is an example: The assessor will give you a different version in the assessment

Improvisation & Interpretation | Example 2

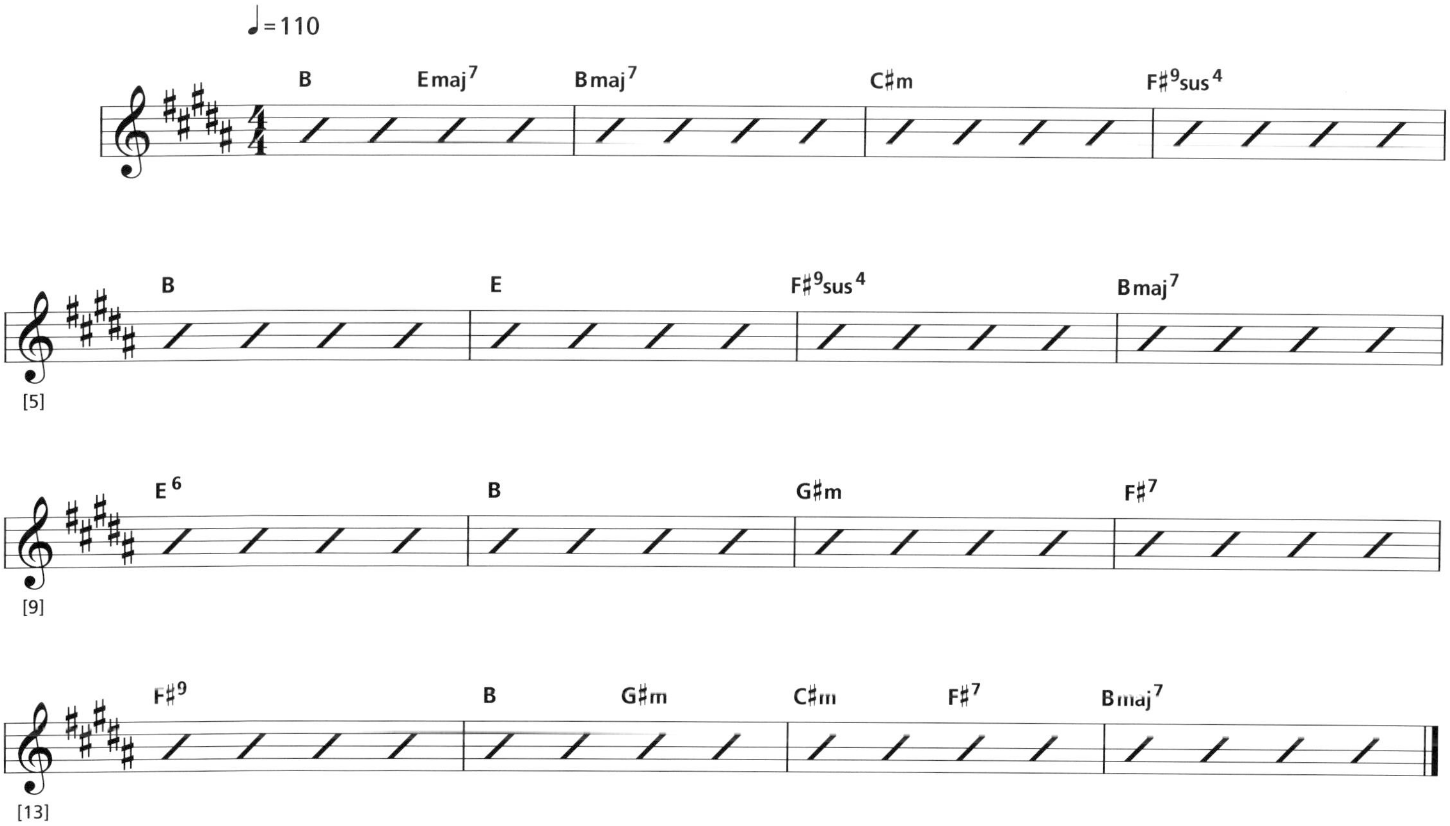

Please note: The test shown is an example: The assessor will give you a different version in the assessment

Ear Tests

In this section, there are two ear tests:

- Melodic Recall
- Harmonic Recall

You will find one example of each type of test printed below and you will need to perform both of them in the assessment.

Test 1: Melodic Recall

The assessor will play you a two measure diatonic melody in the key of C major with a range up to an octave. The first note will be the root note or a fifth. You will hear the test twice, each time with a one measure count-in, then you will hear a further one measure count-in after which you will need to play the melody to the click. The tempo is ♩=95 bpm.

It is acceptable to play over the track as it is being played as well as practising after the second playthough. The length of time available after the second playthrough is pre-recorded on the audio track so the count-in may begin while you are still practising.

Please note: The test shown is an example: The assessor will give you a different version in the assessment

Test 2: Harmonic Recall

The assessor will play you a chord progression containing chords I, II, IV, V, VI in any order or combination in the key of C major. You will hear the chord progression twice, each time with a one measure count-in. You will then hear a further one measure count in before playing back to a click. At this level/grade, seventh chords are introduced. Please note, there is no requirement for the chords to be voicing-specific. The tempo is ♩=95 bpm.

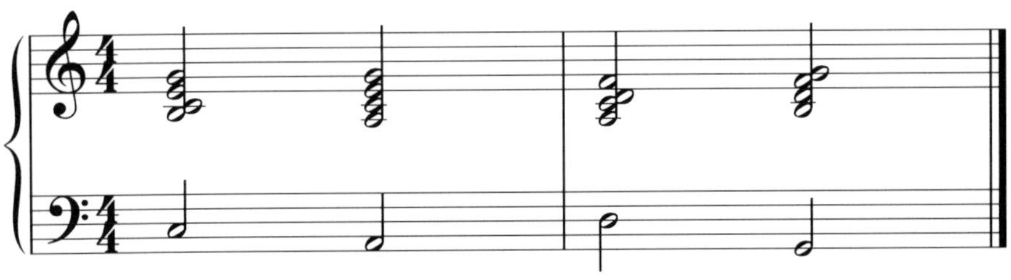

Please note: The test shown is an example: The assessor will give you a different version in the assessment

General Musicianship Questions

The final part of your assessment is the General Musicianship Questions section, which features five questions relating to one of your choice of the performance pieces.

1. You will be asked a question relating to the harmony from a section of one of your pieces
2. You will be asked a question relating to the melody in a section of one of your pieces
3. You will be asked a question relating to the rhythms used in a section of one of your pieces
4. You will be asked a question relating to the technical requirements of one of your pieces
5. You will be asked a question relating to the genre of one of your pieces

Further guidance on the types of questions asked at this level/grade can be found at the RSL website *www.rslawards.com*

Entering Rockschool Assessments

Entering a Rockschool assessment is easy, just go online and follow our simple six step process. All details for entering online, dates, fees, regulations and Free Choice pieces can be found at *www.rslawards.com*

- All candidates should ensure they bring their own Level/Grade syllabus book to the assessment or have proof of digital purchase ready to show the assessor.
- All Level/Grade 6–8 candidates must ensure that they bring valid photo ID to their assessment.

Marking Schemes

Debut to Level/Grade 8

ELEMENT	PASS	MERIT	DISTINCTION
Performance Piece 1	12–14 out of 20	15–17 out of 20	18+ out of 20
Performance Piece 2	12–14 out of 20	15–17 out of 20	18+ out of 20
Performance Piece 3	12–14 out of 20	15–17 out of 20	18+ out of 20
Technical Exercises	9–10 out of 15	11–12 out of 15	13+ out of 15
Sight Reading *or* **Improvisation & Interpretation**	6 out of 10	7–8 out of 10	9+ out of 10
Ear Tests	6 out of 10	7–8 out of 10	9+ out of 10
General Musicianship Questions	3 out of 5	4 out of 5	5 out of 5
TOTAL MARKS	**60%+**	**74%+**	**90%+**

Performance Certificates | Debut to Level/Grade 8

ELEMENT	PASS	MERIT	DISTINCTION
Performance Piece 1	12–14 out of 20	15–17 out of 20	18+ out of 20
Performance Piece 2	12–14 out of 20	15–17 out of 20	18+ out of 20
Performance Piece 3	12–14 out of 20	15–17 out of 20	18+ out of 20
Performance Piece 4	12–14 out of 20	15–17 out of 20	18+ out of 20
Performance Piece 5	12–14 out of 20	15–17 out of 20	18+ out of 20
TOTAL MARKS	**60%+**	**75%+**	**90%+**

Copyright Information

A Thousand Miles
(Carlton)
Universal/MCA Music Limited

Teardrop
(Del Naja/Marshall/Vowles/Fraser)
Universal/Island Music Limited/Sony Music Publishing (UK) Limited

Every Little Thing She Does Is Magic
(Sumner)
G M Sumner

Dangerous
(Robbins/Martin/Guetta/Tuinfort/Evigan)
BMG Rights Management (UK) Limited/Kobalt Music Publishing Limited

Life On Mars?
(Bowie)
RZO Music Limited/EMI Music Publishing Limited/Chrysalis Music Limited

You've Got A Friend In Me (from "Toy Story")
(Newman)
Universal Music Publishing Limited

mcps

Piano Notation Explained

THE MUSICAL STAVE shows pitches and rhythms and is divided by lines into measures. Pitches are named after the first seven letters of the alphabet.

Grace Note: Play the grace note on or before the beat depending on the style of music, then move quickly to the note it leads onto.

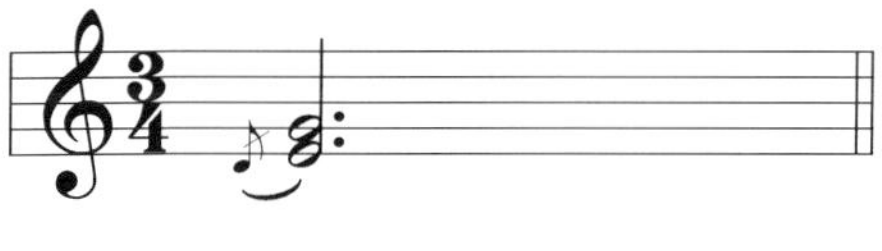

Pedal Marking: Depress and then release the sustain pedal. Multiple pedal operations in a short space of time may be simplified as shown in the last two beats of the measure below.

Spread Chord: Play the chord from the bottom note up (top down only if there is a downward arrow head). The final note should sound by the appropriate notated measure position.

Glissando: Play the notes between the notated pitches by sliding over the keyboard with the fingers or fingernails.

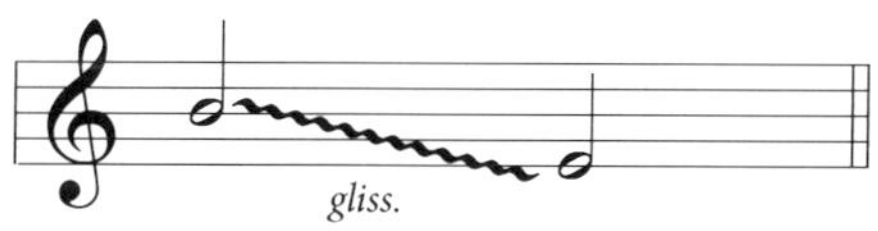

Tremolando: Oscillate at speed between marked notes.

Finger Markings: These numbers represent your fingers. 1 is the thumb, 2 the index finger and so on.

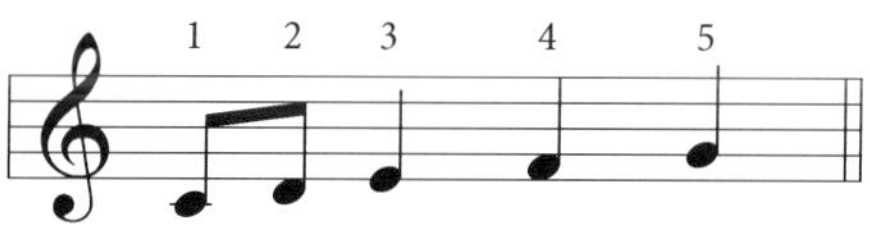

 (accent) • Accentuate note (play it louder).

 (accent) • Accentuate note with great intensity.

 (staccato) • Shorten time value of note.

 (accent) • Accentuate note with more arm weight.

D.𝄋. al Coda • Go back to the sign (𝄋), then play until the measure marked ***To Coda*** 𝄌 then skip to the section marked 𝄌 ***Coda***.

D.C. al Fine • Go back to the beginning of the song and play until the measure marked ***Fine*** (end).

Una Corda • Use soft pedal

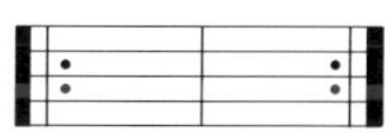 • Repeat the measures between the repeat signs.

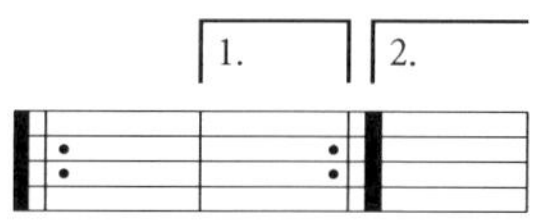

• When a repeated section has different endings, play the first ending only the first time and the second ending only the second time.

rockschool
POPULAR
MUSIC THEORY
The essential guide for rock & pop musicians
Workbook
Workbook
Workbook
Workbook